YOUR HEAD IN MINE

Also by Sasha Moorsom

Perrault's Fairy Tales (1972)
(translated from French)
The Lavender Trip (1976)
In the Shadow of the Paradise Tree (1983)

Also by Michael Young

Labour's Plan for Plenty (1947)
The Rise of the Meritocracy (1957)
Family and Kinship in East London (1957)
(with Peter Willmott)
Family and Class in a London Suburb (1957)
(with Peter Willmott)
The Symmetrical Family (1974)
(with Peter Willmott)
The Elmhirsts of Dartington (1982)
The Metronomic Society (1987)
Life After Work (1991)
(with Tom Schuller)

Sasha Moorsom & Michael Young

YOUR HEAD IN MINE

With an Introduction by Sophie Young

CARCANET

First published in 1994 by
Carcanet Press Limited
208-212 Corn Exchange Buildings
Manchester M4 3BQ

Some of these poems originally appeared in
Dartington Hall News, *Dartington Poetry Anthology*, *London Review of Books*,
New Statesman, and *The Observer*.

A CIP catalogue record for this book
is available from the British Library.
ISBN 1 85754 115 4

The publisher acknowledges financial assistance
from the Arts Council of England

Set in 10pt Joanna by Bryan Williamson, Frome
Printed and bound in England by SRP Ltd, Exeter

Contents

INTRODUCTION
BY SOPHIE YOUNG

My Parents

Michael and Sasha were together for thirty-five years and I am their daughter Sophie, although as a Buddhist nun I was known as Cintāmani. Both my parents wrote poetry throughout their lives, before and during their marriage until my mother's death from cancer in June 1993. When it became apparent that there was no more hope of a cure, one of Sasha's main concerns was to get her poems in order. It makes me both happy and sad that they are now being published. I know how pleased and excited she would have been and I keep wishing I could talk to her, discuss the different poems and how they should be arranged. Reading through them brings her back to life: the clear sound of her voice, her laugh, her presence only just behind the door or around the corner.

The idea of publishing my parents' poems together arose from a comment Sasha made in the last week of her life. My father had just written a poem, 'Cancer', and I asked her what she thought of it. She said it was very good and that it was the other half to her poem, 'Body', which was in a bedside notebook and one of the last she wrote. Looking through her poems after she died I could see how many connections there were with those of Michael. The poems chronicle major themes and events in their lives, often echoing each other, unintentionally perhaps, but all the same they can be seen or heard as complementary reflections. Rather than arranging them in chronological order, it is these echoes that I have tried to listen to in placing the poems where they are in this collection, although other ears may pick up different tunes. Together they seem to weave a kind of pattern reflecting the pattern of their lives – sometimes complementary and unifying, sometimes estranged and far apart, two voices which can sing in harmony or in discord.

My parents were not professional poets, whatever a professional poet may be, but they both used poetry as a medium for expressing particular emotions, conflicts and observations that touched them beneath the skin. The poems come out of ordinary life, the images are accessible and speak to ordinary people. They express the joys and frustrations of bringing up children and letting them go, the approach of middle age, watching their friends and parents die, the ageing process and the passage of time. 'Christopher and the Mountain' is about Michael's mentally disturbed son from his first marriage to Joan. Her death is the subject of a later poem, 'JOAN'. Living and travelling abroad is the background for Sasha's 'Souvenirs of Mauritius' and Michael's 'The Manifesto', about an old man in Botswana. 'After Forty-Five Years' was written when Sasha returned with Michael to South Africa, where she had spent most of her childhood. Nature, the moon, the changing seasons and finally my mother's own illness inspired their poems. They both wrote about animals and Sasha particularly had great empathy with other creatures, an empathy that was also expressed in her pottery and sculpture and that was often manifested in her dreams. Sasha always watched the different birds that came into our garden, making sure there was water for them and food in the winter, banging the window to scare away neighbouring cats. Birds represented to her the singing spirit, the irrepressible calm continuity of nature, the freedom to fly. This comes across very clearly in the last poem of this collection, 'The Company of the Birds', which was read at her funeral.

Where were the poems written? My parents have lived in many houses and travelled through many countries. Although born in Hampshire, Sasha went with her family to South Africa before the war, coming back to England seven years later. She studied English at Cambridge and returned there to live with Michael just before I was born. 'On a Cold Day in Cambridge' was written while she was still a student, as was 'The Estranged Wife' and 'An Academic Remembers'. It was also at Cambridge that she first met Tony White, whose death is referred to much later in the poem 'For Tony'. 'Christopher and the Mountain' and 'The Mountain' were set in North Wales where Michael's mother had a cottage. We lived for some years in Bethnal Green where the early poems about being a mother were written. It was there that Sasha met the old lady 'Miss Martin' and Michael, working there many years later, wrote 'Neighbours'. Next came a long stretch in Highgate, interspersed with periods abroad in Mauritius and Africa. In 1977 we moved to Dartington in Devon where Sasha wrote 'Cold April', 'Verbiage' and 'Summer Morning'. At the same time as I joined the monastery my parents moved back to London. It was here that all the later poems were written, 'Cityscape', 'Strip-Tease', 'The Metronomic Moon' and the ones about death and Sasha's illness. She died in her own bed at home, in their house in Islington where Michael continues to live. There is a lot more that could be said about the significance of these places in their lives but this is a poetic record and not a biography.

Poetry was important to Sasha from an early age. While a young student at Cambridge she wrote in her diary:

> The community of spirit I feel with people when I'm reading them

is really most painful. I am them. I love them as much as anyone I know. I feel as if I could conjure them up in my room, by strength of will. Is this the only immortality?

She kept a journal for many years and when first in hospital having treatment for cancer she wrote about her lifetime's reading of poetry:

> I have a longing to have all the poems I love most in a little book. When I get home I'll try to get them copied and put them all together. But who would I ask to do it if I can't walk properly? I have such a dread of having to ask people to do every little thing for me. Cutting down on any wantings is the only answer, as the Buddhist monks and nuns learn to do. One can manage with very little. Only I do long for the poems. But I'm afraid they'll make me cry too.

Six months later, while undergoing chemotherapy, there is another entry in her diary:

> The invisible worm in Blake's poem 'O Rose thou art sick…' seems like a perfect metaphor for cancer. I wrote a poem about the blood-red door across the square ['Cityscape']. Left it on Michael's pillow last night. He liked it but queried one line which we then discussed for a while, reflecting on how much weight attaches to every word in a poem, how crucial each bit is. Maybe that's why I like poetry so much.

Creativity manifests itself in myriad ways and my parents have not been limited to writing poetry. Michael has written many books as a sociologist and biographer, while Sasha had two novels published, two works she translated from French and many articles as a freelance journalist. They both loved painting and Sasha took this further in sculpture and ceramics. She even wrote music, composing a beautiful song that was performed for the first time at her funeral. Three days before she died my mother did a pastel drawing of a flower arrangement at the foot of her bed, flowers brought from the monastery by some of my fellow nuns. The drawing is so full of life and colour that it is hard to believe how close she was to death. She died the way that she lived, with grace and dignity, expressing her deepest nature and appreciation of life in ways that others could share.

Sasha would sometimes use poetry to communicate in a more subtle way that which was difficult to talk about directly. This was the case with 'The Green Stone' which was written for two friends who had also recently left the monastic life, Mary and Kittisaro. On their last visit they had given her a green stone which she found very calming to hold in moments of pain or distress. This was just at the time when the second round of chemotherapy was stopped because it wasn't doing her any good. She knew then that she was dying. One evening after returning home from the hospital for the last time she showed me this poem. I read it sitting on her bed and realized that through these few lines of poetry she was telling me that she would soon be going and could accept with infinite sadness and yet peace this transformation of flesh to ashes. My eyes filled with tears and as we looked at each other there was an understanding deeper than any words could go.

When I first shaved my head and entered the monastery Sasha wrote a poem, 'For my Daughter on her Becoming an Anagarika'. Anagarika means 'homeless one' in the Buddhist language of Pali, a novice making the initial year-long commitment to monastic life. I am sorry that her feeling at the time was that I had chosen 'a childless road of abnegation' but her attitude to my being a nun changed a lot over the years as I too changed, and our relationship became increasingly harmonious and loving. It was when she first became ill that I began to feel myself drawn back to the world I had left behind ten years before. The realization of her mortality brought a growing awareness of my own limited life span. There was an indefinable sense that I would be needed outside the confines of monastic life, to take on family responsibilities and learn to live peacefully in the crazy modern world. However it was a difficult decision to make and it was almost a year before I actually disrobed. This time it was my father who, on seeing me in ordinary clothes again, was moved to write a poem, 'My Daughter is Leaving her Monastery'.

There was a kind of completion in being able to share with my mother those last few months of her life, to care for her as a daughter and not as a nun. We said how glad we were and how lucky to have had the opportunity in our lifetimes to reach such a resolution and closeness between us. As her body became weaker it was as if she was passing on her strength and vitality to me and I was passing on to her the peace I had found from the contemplative life of a nun. Death is the greatest loss but it can also be a gift if we know how to receive it.

YOUR HEAD IN MINE

Asthma

When the other boys dared me to crawl first
Through the tunnel the farmer had left,
Head down, I soon forgot the barbs of straw
Pricking the sweat from my runneled back.
All at once I was gulping in a tomb,
The light shut out behind my head,
With only automated knees propelling me through the dark,
As I fell towards the pinpoint of air at the other end
I had almost been drowned by a haystack.

M.Y. (1978)

Expulsion

For fourteen years I moved through time like someone
Walking in water, the least ripple gone
To merge into the next before it was begun.

So everything was now, and I, submerged,
Fed on it and knew no separation,
Till waters churned and this raw sea-creature emerged.

Horses grazing on shore shied in surprise
But one, submissive, took me on its back.
The world began to turn before my new-born eyes.

At first we walked slowly, discovering;
My clumsy fingers held the halter slack,
Always above my head were sea-birds, hovering.

But as we left the sea and rode inland
The narrow pathway broadened to a road
The rope slid harshly through my useless hand.

With eyeballs rolling and its ears laid low
The horse galloped until my long hair flowed
Like seaweed that the roaring waters drag in tow.

Behind me streams the future as I ride
Try as I may there is no turning back;
No-one is strong enough to stand against this tide.

What can I do but shut my eyes and love
This whirling motion that is called the world
And make my element the earth on which I move?

For now even the sea fills me with fear,
If back into its waters I was hurled
How could I breathe in that dark sublunary sphere?

S.M. (1960)

The Mountain

This evening the clouds kidnapped so much sea again
Ambition could not blow them higher than the peak.
Where that dark plumber waited to drill their load.
When the unbound waters leapt for home
From our windows we could see the whiteness
Of the veins which stood out from his arms
And hear the small stones cracking in his fists.

M.Y. (1959)

Christopher and the Mountain

When the rolling tentacles of mist
Reach down the slopes of the mountain
And float through the window behind his head
To touch his beard with grey,
Chris stands listening to his long fingers
Reaching down the covers of the chair.
'There are boys and girls,' he said,
'Can you guess correctly
How many there were in the secret garden?'

M.Y. (1959)

At a Distance

Across the park I see my daughter walking
Pigeon-toed, holding someone else's hand.
Behind her, dragging a broken stick, her brother.
Seen unexpectedly like this at a distance they seem
Surprisingly small and fragile.

Where are those screeching monsters who pursue me
Demanding drinks, a handkerchief, a story,
Following me even into the lavatory
Where they sprawl quarrelling on the mat?

Their presence filling my days, even my dreams,
Has dislocated me into being a mother.
Trying to catch up with a role
I never guessed would throw me out like that
I seem to be always running.

This distance brings me to a sudden halt
Jerking me back to a forgotten self
Who can watch with affection and a quiet detachment
Two children crossing the grass.

S.M. (1966)

Nail-Biter

Perhaps these hands express the conflict best.
They must be always poised ready
To wipe noses, dishes, bottoms,
Catch someone falling, do up a difficult button,
Soothe, stroke. Do they want to?
Sometimes the longing to scratch, slap
As hard as they can, push and pinch,
Strangle, possesses them. What can I do?
Bite them. My nails are ugly, you complain.
At least the skin I have torn is mine, not yours.

S.M. (1967)

Mothering

Sometimes at night I wake up in a sweat,
Tense at a vision of destruction
Of flesh frail as strawberries
Skulls light and crushable as shells.
Their skin, so much more delicate than ours,
A subtle casing for their flowering,
Bruising as easily as a petal on the stones.

Rigid in darkness gripping the bed,
My eyes open to a silent room.
That scream was in my head, gone with the dream,
But not the fear. My throat aches with it.
Prowling the passage I stop inside each room,
See for myself their quiet, sleeping bodies
Ghostly in stillness. Are their spirits here?

And then the dream's unravelling begins.
This horror is a horror I must own,
It comes from me. My fear engenders it,
Or so they say, those who interpret dreams.
A fear of what? Of sudden accident?
Not from outside, the fear is of myself,
The damage I might do, not veiled in dreams,
Not to their sleeping but their waking selves.

S.M. (1968)

Cold April

Late snow coming
A white cloud of destruction,
Unpredictable.
All yesterday with such care we settled
Each tiny plant
Snugly in its bed of peat and loam
Or lime or horse manure,
According to need,
The nature of the seed determining
What soil should succour it.
Singing inside you were, kneeling in a
Sunday posture of reverence.

Today the moor is dredged with snow.
From my window
I watch their small green faces
Vanish in whiteness as the snow-flakes fall
Faster and faster.
Like our children now they are
Outside, beyond our care
Though not our caring.
What good's anxiety, fretting or fussing?
The planting's over.
We can't predict
What storms will rage
Nor how they may survive.

S.M. (1978)

For my Daughter
on her Becoming an Anagarika

I pass my hand over your shaven head
As rough as sandpaper, feeling the bump
Where nineteen years ago you wedged
In some dark passage of my uterus.
It was a difficult birth, as this is.
Your new white robes recall the first white garment
We wrapped you in just after you were born.
I lay in ecstasy, holding you in my arms.

You have chosen now
To rise at four, to eat one meal a day,
Own nothing but these robes,
Lie on a hard low mattress on the floor
Among the homeless ones, the wanderers.

Silently they eat, silently sit
In meditation.
The evening chanting in the flickering light
Of candles – Buddha, Dhamma, Sangha –
Gravelly voices of the droning monks
Lead you along a path I cannot follow
I could not know I laboured so that you
Might choose this childless road of abnegation.

S.M. (1982)

My Daughter is Leaving her Monastery

She must have hitched up the skirts of her brown robe
And stuffed them into her new trousers to show me.
Hers were no ordinary trousers
They were more womanly than the skirts.
They were silky and black and white
Worked into a mazy pattern like trailing leaves.
They were pleated at the waist and
Billowed sideways from her hips like bamboos bending to the
wind.

She smiled and asked 'Do you like them?'
'Yes, I like them,' I said.
After eleven years, time enough for the wind to blow,
I know now my daughter is disrobing.

M.Y. (1992)

In the Handy Afternoon

In the handy afternoon we labour
Sowing seeds of love in uneven furrows.
We get up to welcome the evening
And prowl about under the stars with lifted faces.
So may the sun bless our procreation
And the moon be our goddess of meditation.

S.M. (1956)

Mirage

A dead waste lies between us, dry and bare,
And if I suddenly see water shimmering
A blue haze in the distance and drag myself
Across that burnt-out place, crawling in dust
To drown a thirst that chokes me like a gag,
Proximity proves it only another mirage –
Just so much more dry sand between the fingers.

The space all round is frightening. Shall I just
Lie down here quietly shutting my eyes
And let the sand shift slowly up my sides
Across my back, until it covers me,
Nothing left except the faintest mound?
I don't think now I could get up again
To reach for it if there were really water.

S.M. (1955)

On a Cold Day in Cambridge

Inside the cage of my head
I tread the wheel like a frantic mouse
Getting nowhere.
How can I escape going over
The same scenes,
Hearing the same phrases spoken again and again
But out of context
So that the meaning I give them may not be
The meaning you intended?

Words blow about
Spoken not at random but flown as kites
To circulate
In unknown currents of air. Once launched they veer
Out of control
Flap like distraught birds to collide with each other
Breaking the thread
That linked them at a distance
To your guiding hand.

Intention is not everything.
We can only intend
What we know about our feelings.
What we do not know
Insinuates itself in spite of us
Starting these slow
Reverberating ripples from explosions
No seismograph
Can measure, nor we hope to understand.

S.M. (1952)

The Estranged Wife

I do not like your way of leave-taking.
If it could only be
'Goodbye, I'm off' or even, 'This is the end.'
I'd know, then, what to expect better than this
Trial separation of estrangement.
You've left behind a lot of books, some shoes,
An old coat in the hall.
Outposts of what?
An intention, perhaps, to return,
Homing devices to bring you circling back
Like a bird that hovers over a familiar field
Wondering if the pickings are better here than he remembered?

It's still the same old patch of grass
Thin, in places, not offering much
That's new. Don't they say, farmers,
That such and such a plot is exhausted now,
Needs to lie fallow, to have the ground
Ploughed in, nothing expected of it?
I'd like that chance,
To know the hawk has gone, his watchful eye
Turned in other directions. A final parting.
That could be the start
Of trying to grow again something like love.

S.M. (1953)

An Academic Remembers

You offered me something none of the others did,
Examining the smallest mole on my upper arm
To bless it with your tongue,
Not your mind, you said, who cares about your mind?
It's your body I'm after.
After, after noons, after drinking, laughter,
No-one ever found me so absurd.

Now sagging, crinkled, memories of betrayals
Stacked like card indexes in my head
As I thumb through
The endless arguments over intention,
What-do-we-mean-by-what-did-he-really-mean-by?

All those discussions
Unpicking other men's theories like
Fine stitching under a magnifying glass,
A perfect paradigm of aggression,
Kant, Wittgenstein, Popper, reduced
To a gerrymandering of verbal tricks.
All cant to me now, remembering
The laughter you smothered in my armpits.

S.M. (1953)

Images

That image caught in the glass
Accidentally as I cross the room –
Can I bear to face it any more?
The same glare, same set mouth,
Eyes more weary
With each late night of introspection
Into the small hours,
Reading of others' journeys into the same unknown,
Nel mezzo del cammin di nostra vita
An endless refrain in my head.

Suspended in these middle years
Not balanced but teetering on some edge
Backwards and forwards,
I look behind at the landmarks of failure,
Of love I did not give,
The spaces between hands
Stretched out but not reaching each other,
At extinct volcanoes of anger
Whose white-hot lava once
Turned others' gestures to stone as well as mine.

Backwards the mind's telescope
Miniaturises through the inverted lens
A whole Pompeii of human images
Visible only to myself, quite still
In a landscape where time has stopped.
Forwards everything is movement, shouting how
Age is not a slow decline, a stumbling down the years,
But the wind tunnel of time
Sucking us faster and faster
Into silence.

S.M. (1976)

The Dialectic

The rage of each wave is not spent
Until, put into reverse,
It streams back down the beach,
And hissing to the last
Throws the pebbles and itself against the next.
But between them, the advance and the recoil,
The ever-innovating cartographic double tongue
Licks salt-white upon the impressed sand the film of Wales,
Of France, of continents known and as yet unknown.

With this reminder the recoiling wave admits,
What the sand-maps do not assert,
That the other's force is greater,
That the coasts themselves have been indented
Because each incoming wave
Has a youthful strength greater in the end
Than the hissful clawing back of age.

M.Y. (1987)

Fire or Water

Again I see the ghost in Regent's Park
Scattering her wishes on the water
Each wish an ash
Each wish her own.

She had not wanted to die by water
She wanted to die by fire
To burn so fiercely
The lake would become vapour as well.

But as the flames consume her
The ash on the water, glowing for a moment,
Breathes its little puff of smoke
Before it sinks beneath the surface.

I saw the ghost in Regent's Park
Alchemised into ashes on the water
Her ashes wishes
Her wishes drowned.

M.Y. (1983)

Souvenirs of Mauritius

1 *Dog, Sub-Tropical Island Species*

Dogs everywhere
They lie half in the road – asleep or dead?
Move, if they do,
Slowly, without energy, reactions dulled
To a limping, last-minute evasion of passing cars
Not always in time –
That brown one's paw dangles like a crushed twig,
Below her bitch's belly
Dugs flap like a row of thin hot-water bottles
Perished from too much use
As she noses among fish bones in the gutter.

On this island
Dogs are beggars who dare not even beg,
No place for them
To fawn on affluence
Living as they do on the leftovers
Of people who have nothing left over
Themselves scavengers
Themselves, on occasion, cringing,
Themselves with the slow movements of perpetual hunger.

Behind the huts
One howls all night long
The sound throbbing through darkness
Monotonously,
A complaint that has no ending.
Dogs howl
Where people have no voice.

S.M. (1971)

2 *A Short Walk down Royal Road*

We never saw ourselves before as
White.
Whiter than white, Blue Magic bleached,
Albino, like things
Uncovered by an upturned stone
Disgusting in their pallor.

Down the street dark faces, black to golden,
A soft vibration from skins
Magnetised towards sunlight,
Mercurial colours
Of children like darting tropical birds.
It's not what they show
In their bright indifferent eyes
That fixes the image,
It's merely the reflection of ourselves –
Eyes like mirrored glass in which, minutely,
We see ourselves walking.
The self-disgust is ours, not theirs.

And so, perhaps, is all self-consciousness,
A throwing back of the image
Slap in the face,
Longing to be inside some other skin,
Uncertain of our own identity,
Occasioned by being in a world of colours
Where white is the nothing of colour.

S.M. (1971)

3 *The Orphanage Outing at Tamarin Beach*

Nuns delicate nuns
Nuns like white birds
Fluttering under the trees
Long-tailed gulls
Smudged brown at the face
Pecking up children like scattered crumbs
As they stray towards the water

There is a tide here that drowns people
So the nuns hover
With small soft cries of sea birds
Protecting
Between the tamarind trees and the water
While the waves swell and break
Onto a beach where the children will walk
Alone one day in a world where nuns
Have no jurisdiction
But later much later

S.M. (1971)

The Manifesto

That heap of rags, not there before we left,
Which seems to have grown like a fungus from the African earth,
Speaks through a stick once green upon a tree
Which is now scathed white by age and use.
This creature with hidden head,
With no legs to walk with,
Or voice to talk with,
By rolling the stick slowly forwards through the dust
With two black fingers protruding from the mound of cloth,
Bone upon wood, wood upon earth,
Declares that as the stick had been a tree,
With a staff to lean on
He had been a man.

M.Y. (1974)

After Forty-Five Years

Cape Ghost Frogs tap at the windows all night long,
'Tap, tap, we want to come in,' they are saying, 'tap, tap.
We are the ghosts of children who once stayed here,
Who swung on the beams, raced down to the brown water,
Pushing our boats through the weeds among white-nosed coots
While the cormorants rose with great flapping of black wings.'
The day comes. Overhead, buzzards soar and dip
In a cloudless sky above the swaying gum trees.
The ghost frogs go back up the mountain to sleep in the Disas
But I will remember the children who used to stay here
In the cottage by the vlei. I am still one of them.

S.M. (1991)

Visiting the Lake District

Coming back to his native fells
After a gap of nearly fifty years
My father seems possessed.

The houses where he visited as a child
Have signs for 'Bed and Breakfast. Vacancies'.
We stay in one and munching our cold toast
Look out on a croquet lawn jumping with rabbits.
Each morning sharp at half-past nine we start
On some minutely charted expedition
The contours mapped, unchanging, in his mind.

He leaps up rocks like one of those shaggy rams
We startle unexpectedly on a crag,
Wild eyes staring towards a view
We ought to see if only the mist would lift.
Down in the valleys he prowls round empty churches
Stripping the ivy from derelict tombstones
To peer at a name he remembers – some long-dead relative.

It triggers off an endless family history
I try to be interested in. One grave where a loose
Panel of stone seemed to be coming away
Had him excitedly shoving at the edge
As if he wanted to get at the bones inside.
He strokes an urn. 'I'd like to take this with me.
It would look well on the terrace at home, don't you think?'

I don't understand his yearning for these relics.
Is it because he feels
Much more at home with them, now, than with us?

S.M. (1974)

Not Sound Proof

Upstairs on heavy feet my father laboriously
Prepares for bed
Collects his chamber pot, lays out a tray
With honey and Frugrains for his breakfast.
He winds his watch and places it nearby
Ready to be consulted in case of insomnia,
Sets his electric-blanket thermostat
And switches it on. Gets into bed
Then out again for a final pee.

This much I guess.
The others mutter crossly,
'What on earth can he be doing
Bumbling about like that for hours on end?'
'I'll go and see.'
But when I climb the stairs
I find him stretched out gravely on the bed
Transistor still plugged murmuring to his ear
The lights all blazing where he lies asleep.

S.M. (1979)

The Smiling Woman

I often stood to watch them
Etched against the windows
Climbing, coughing, up the stairs
Leaning, tired, against the railings
Wearing bed-worn clothes, the same by night and day,
Sometimes when I shouted
They cupped their hands to their ears
They could hear but not answer
They moved their lips
But no sound came out
They left no tell-tale smell behind them
They were always stumbling, doggedly, up and down stairs

Once, hurrying along the street
I caught up with one of their women
She stopped and seemed to see me
When I asked her who she was
It all became clear
Although she did not answer
Her creases broke into a smile
Which seemed to come from far within and grow
This was her answer.
She was not dead like us.
She was still alive; she could smile.

M.Y. (1975)

Miss Martin

I hardly recognise you crossing the road.
Bent double over your stick, your eyes on my feet,
Wondering who blocks your way, whose hand on your shoulder,
You clutch me down, my straight back bent like yours
So, for a moment, I know your endless pain.
My face twists to see into yours
As I crouch, child-high, on the pavement
Searching for the remembered blue of your eyes
In mists of watering grey.

You ask what time it is – late evening surely?
When you hear I've only just had breakfast
Confusion sets your frail shoulders trembling:
The whole of a day still left to crawl through.
You open your blistered hands, show me the sores
On your shrivelled leg where you dragged yourself to the bed
After you fell, saying, it's the tablets
They give me too many tablets, shaking your head.
My ears drown with your sadness, I cannot move,
Witness to the decay that tortures your body
While my mouth jabbers meaningless comfort.

S.M. (1965)

Rhesus Monkeys

When that small mouse set off deliberately
Whirring its click-clack course across the floor
Into the laboratory among the monkeys,
Chattering in fright they leapt away from it
To clutch, shivering, at their mothers' rocking breasts.

Just as we had expected; we noted it down:
'In moments of stress the baby rhesus monkey
Will cling to its towelling foster-mother for comfort.'
Towelling on rockers. This is the best they know,
Preferring it to the other model of wire,
Milk bottles dangling where the nipples should be;
To these they venture only when hunger drives them,
Then back to the towelling to rock themselves asleep.

From behind glass we order their environment,
Arrange experiments that are called controlled,
Split up families, feed them, give them frights,
Provide a simulated comforter.
Their quick bright eyes look round in puzzlement,
Stare out at us as we stare in at them
Except (of course) the glass is one way only.
To our advantage.

And we, in turn, as night falls
Beyond the laboratory windows, our watching ended,
Switch off the daylight in their stuffy room
And turn towards a sky that offers us only
Darkness, our bright eyes staring into it.

S.M. (1970)

The Shark Caller of Kontu, New Guinea

Like two-toned submarines, white bellied,
They cruise below the surface effortlessly
As sunlight ripples through the water
On gleaming grey impermeable skin.

Above in his flimsy boat the small brown man
Skims the water with his paddle,
Shaking his rattle of coconut shells
Till it cries out like a fish in distress,
Magic dissimulating cries
To draw the sharks towards him.

All week he has prepared himself,
Not sleeping with his wife,
Not treading on shit of pigs or flying foxes,
Waiting for the dream that tells him when to go.

On this particular morning
He wakes up knowing the time has come.
Out in the shallow lagoon he catches bait-fish
Then spears the reef again and again
Clanging metal on rock to tell the sharks
The time is now, now is the time to appear.

His voice cries over the water like a sea-bird's,
'The high tide's coming, let it bring the big fish with it.
Swim towards me, fish, I'm ready for you, swim,
Maroa has created sharks and the magic to catch them.'

Over this bridge of magic he floats
Towards the spirit sharks,
Dropping stones in the water one by one
To tell them he's coming. Six stones
Fall to the sea-bed, one by one by one
Marking his passage out into the bay.

With held breath he angles the wooden propeller
Baited with delicacies over the edge of the boat
And waits for a shadow to nose its way upwards.
The rope snare trembles ready in his hand.

With one thrust the noose locks round its jaw.
The shark jerks and twists,
Thrashing the water with its tail,
As it fights to free itself with the blade spinning
Round and around and around in a frenzy of foam.
The man clings on, tightening the rope like a vice.

His hands drip blood as he hauls the fish over the side.
It cannot bite him, cannot utter shark-cries,
Imprisoned in cord it falls like wet stone at his feet.
The man clubs it to death.

He raises his conch-shell and blows
A call full of sea-wind and the sound of triumph.
'This is the way we ask Maroa for help.
Only if he wills it will the shark be caught,
Will rain fall, will the taro grow,
Will we be at one with our universe.'

S.M. (1975)

Lemurs of Madagascar

You seem outraged that I should be
So much in love with lemurs.
What about people, you ask, the poor people
The island is full of?

Ah but it's their difference that attracts me
To lemurs; they have other exigencies
Than us, can leap and fly, eat cyanide, besides
They are night creatures, gleaning the forest canopy
Under cover of darkness with mournful fluting.

And when day comes
They sit with arms outstretched on a clump of rocks
Baring their chests, like furry Bodhisattvas
To meditate in the sun.

S.M. (1987)

Seagulls in Night Formation

There they were this morning, those gulls
I had so often seen and heard before
Fantailing, banking, sharply wheeling
Screaming fiercely as they dive-bombed
Each for each, not for each other
Sharp yellow beaks glinting
Before upending into the sewery water
To gobble up the outfall sludge

There they were tonight, the same gulls
All grace now
Not battling and breasting against the air
But sailing serenely in the slow formation
Of a glide-borne diamond
Each joined invisibly to each around
Oh, a centre bird with grey-tipped wings
Shining straight into my inner eye.

M.Y. (1986)

Summer Morning

Birds go about their business
Regardless of my sorrow or yours,
Fly-catcher darting after gnats,
Snub-tailed wren pouring out its
Liquid epithalamium
Early, early in the morning when
Sunlight first slants sideways through
The ash branches
And the long sleepless night is over.

S.M. (1979)

Dog Rose

A dog rose baring itself to a bee
Is what I'm like when you come into the room.
Oh what a nuzzling for honey goes on, bumbling through stamens,
Past pollen-heavy antlers, round sticky filaments,
To reach the nectary.

Bees hover and depart. That is their nature.
But I wish
Summer did not have to end
With falling of petals,
All that sweet searching over.

S.M. (1968)

Games of Middle-Age

Crouched, like a humped animal, listening
In bushes at the end of the garden to cries of
'Coming. I counted a hundred. Ready?'
Shrill screams of discovery,
Then savage feet pounding along the path
As the wolf-he gobbles up the scattered flock.

The elaborate rules involve us mercilessly
In their specialised deceptions.
Plump legs in jeans dash over the lawn
To lurk behind the greenhouse where kissing can be
Prolonged and invisible,
Or two squash in a cupboard,
Tennis rackets pressed along their thighs
While balls, dislodged, go ping, pong, on the strings.
Only spoil-sports don't play.

So we set free
The rages of our sober daylight selves
Allowing, in one short evening,
Lust, hidden for years,
For someone else's mate, to surface
In the long wet grass beyond the orchard.

Lights out. Games are better in the dark.
Only in that top window where children sleep
A night-light flickers, casting its tiny glow
On faces of perfect, innocent composure
Dreaming of
Hide and seek that's only hide and seek.

S.M. (1970)

The Farewell Party

Can I introduce you to Elena?
Says our host, his arm linked to hers.
She shakes hands with me and smiles,
Seeming not to share the secret
That more than our hands have touched before.

Can she not remember
The ledge above the waves before she stopped my ears,
The grass under the stars before she shut my eyes,
The icy bedroom in an Exeter hotel
Before she drew the curtains against the night?

Smoothing her purple dress over her hips as she used to do,
She turns away and smiles at the next man.
She who had power to plug my ears and close my eyes
Can now stop off my past by not acknowledging hers.
You should not have introduced me to this Elena.

M.Y. (1985)

The Moon at Sharpham

When I woke up from my twitching sleep
Its light was in the room.
I knelt by the window and looked up,
Remembering the day's news in the paper
That a Russian rocket has circled
The side I cannot see
And photographed its hidden continents.

My own continent is here.
The shape of trees, hedges and hills
Are luminous behind the haze.
The tractor has stopped.
All that moves down by the water
Are ripples of mist
Riding barely faster than the tide.

The earth men are drinking coffee
To keep themselves awake
In their observatories on top of the Urals.
We moon men cannot sleep,
We peer, dazed, from windows
And bump against dustbins
With our pyjama legs.

M.Y. (1964)

Strip-Tease

There she is,
There she is, the old moon,
There she is, with her face creamed for the night,
Hardly worth a bedtime look,
Until suddenly, like a horse released from the starting gate,
She leaps across my alerted eyes,
Catapulted forward by the racing cloud,
As if it were not the cloud but she by me
Who had been panicked into girlish flight.

When, to tantalise, she sheds the cloud,
Her strip tease is not for me.
She is not waiting, naked and motionless, for me to capture
Her exits and entrances into my auditorium
But for the unseeing stars to regain their sight.

M.Y. (1983)

For Tony

Keep going to the window, stare at the night sky,
Full moon all this week.
Red flashes of planes disappear into darkness
Like the tail-lights of cars on a windy highway.
Knowing the looking is hopeless, how can I stop
Trying to locate you somewhere?

I wish I did not have this ear for voices.
When you rang, hullo was all you had to say
And I knew, to your pretended surprise,
Who it was. Hullo, hullo,
Your voice is sounding in my head continuously.
Hullo. My shout, however loud, vanishes into the sky.

Did you know how passionately you were loved,
Guru-routier, friend to so many of us,
Magus who linked such disparate spirits,
Master of transformations,
Anything still possible in your presence?
Declarations would have embarrassed you.
People are so afraid of feeling, you said,
Including yourself in that fear.
Now feeling drowns us, more than we can bear.

If this had happened any other time
It would have been you we turned to.
How can you comfort us for your own death?
A common grief. Does that make it worse?
It seems to. No shared ritual with any meaning.
You leave us locked in private desolation,
Rock-a-by babies on the tree top,
Going to fall, going to fall, afraid,
Wanting to be in your company.

S.M. (1976)

Verbiage

I do not exist
Just one of those walking mouths
Out of which sounds come
That simulate emotion.

But you answer
As if you thought there really was
Somebody there
To surprise with the seriousness
Of your replies.
Who is it you are talking to?

I have gone into No-man's-land
Where there is no direction
Weightless, floating in a cold void,
No measure, nothing growing,
Just voice in air sounding
A rigmarole of pain.

Take no notice
Of this walking mouth
Out of which pain comes
That simulates words
It does not exist.

S.M. (1978)

My Father

Did so much of you have to die at once?
It could have been your nose.
That might have been for the good.
Or your fingernails
I wouldn't have minded that.
But why your eyes, and your bristling moustache,
Your fingers that grasped your baton,
Your hand that held it up against the light
Showed grainy red veins branching out like a tree,
Why your feet with your inching toes,
And why, oh why, did your voice have to die,
Trailing away and then falling to silence.

M.Y. (1973)

Flowers for my Mother, Dying

My hands have time to twist like yours,
Gnarled Bonsai trees, brown
Blotches of lichen on the skin
So paper-thin, a fragile bark of tissue.

My legs have time to shrink like yours,
Brittle as dried stems bleached
White with age,
Buckling at the knees with the least pressure;

And my head to fill with confused dreams
Where the long-dead walk in the door, seeming
More real than the living,
And you smile and say, 'The flowers have come,'
As the room fills with their scent.

S.M. (1991)

Jewels in my Hand

I hold dead friends like jewels in my hand
Watching their brilliance gleam against my palm
Turquoise and emerald, jade, a golden band.

All ravages of time they can withstand
Like talismans their grace keeps me from harm
I hold dead friends like jewels in my hand.

I see them standing in some borderland
Their heads half-turned, waiting to take my arm
Turquoise and emerald, jade, a golden band.

I'm not afraid they will misunderstand
My turning to them like a magic charm
I hold dead friends like jewels in my hand
Turquoise and emerald, jade, a golden band.

S.M. (1992)

Dialling Death

Will mankind's next scientific advance
By another miracle of communication
Install satellite phones in every home
To jump the barrier between the before and after
Into the unknown territory on the other shore
From where no reliable message has come before?

If we find galactic colonies already there
With regular bulletins on the hour
From the newsrooms of the Other World Service
Augmenting the private lines to our departed,
The first people ever to know our fate
We will no longer need to speculate.

Let us hope Thou wilt not be there as well
To cut off all the lines except the one
To Thine own ear
Let us pray that Thou
Wilt not be tempted to answer back
In Thy mercy keep in everlasting doubt
The secret of our Kingdom and Thy clout.

M.Y. (1985)

Football

As he runs clear
I too am alone.
I turn away my eyes
To watch the vibration in the crowd
Shot from some hidden spring of joy
Shape itself into a wave,
Reach out as if to lick the player's feet and
Like a wind tumbling the stems of grass
Bend each body before its surge
Until it breaks the frontmost row
Against the barrier.

The three black policemen
Must have heard some cry
Like a bird's against the gale.
They too turn away from the play,
Climb the fence and
Lifting high into the air a boy
With a white face under a bobbled hat
Carry him slowly along the by-line.
When the roar crescendos again
He struggles to raise his head,
Then falls back and is still.

M.Y. (1954)

JOAN

The police officer standing above her will never know
Her mouth used to twitch so much
(Julia, Oscar, Arthur, Norman)
For Joan is peaceful now
Her face will never feel cold again
(No marks on her body)
The only marks the marks of age
(Born October 4, 1917)
There will be no more postponements
(Over and out)
As his radio continues to crackle
Her expression is as eager as when she was a girl.

M.Y. (1991)

Cityscape

I fear the blood-red door across the square
Bleeding into the car in front of it.
At night shouts from the pub at closing time,
The lullaby of sirens, manic laughter,
The girls who shriek as if they're being raped,
Wind me up for the restless hours ahead.

Last night at three o'clock a chilling cry
Woke me so suddenly I leapt to the wooden shutters,
Opened them, looked out, could see nothing,
Asking myself if the cry was dreamt or real.

Today I hear of a man stabbed in a gaming club
Who crawled the length of the street looking for help.
He must have been camouflaged by that car.

Should I have gone out there in my nightdress
Searching the dog-shit pavements till I found him?
Instead I closed the shutters, crept to bed,
Tried to climb my way back to that calm ledge of sleep
But lay awake, not dreaming, listening.

S.M. (1992)

The Metronomic Moon

In other years I would say, how pretty they are,
The cherries outside our house.
This autumn I see the first leaves
Writhe from the green into the yellow and
From the yellow into what seems a frantic red
Before they corkscrew to their conclusion
When the morning wipers scrape them from the windscreens
To drop them in the dog shit on the pavement.
Their beauty has not brought them mercy.

The cherry flaunting first and shedding fastest
Flies a few prayer flags in tatters.
When the time is ripe (soon now)
The metronomic moon on cue will let slip
The north wind to bite the branches bare and
Lay out the bony tree against the back-lit tombgrey sky.
In other years I would say, how lucky we are,
The people inside our house.
But the luck has not brought us mercy.

M.Y. (1991)

Some Things…

Some things are too sad to recognise.
Stubbing your toe against them like a stone in the dark
The unexpected pain drops you to your knees.
Get up. Go on. Keep walking.
Next time look where you're going.

S.M. (1975)

Women's Ward

This is a hard country to understand
I fell into it unexpectedly
Without map or guide, no language preparation,
Here in this bed, one among thirty women
Crippled with pain. Can't turn over,
Can't sit up. White-coated doctors
Stand at the end of the bed muttering
Incomprehensible syllables.
The walking wounded creep towards the sluice
Carrying their handbags full of piss;
Across the ward a girl is screaming non-stop
In the agony of sickle-cell anaemia;
From my neighbour's nose green bile
Seeps down a tube while there in the corner,
With curtains drawn, a woman is slowly dying
Her fading moans and calls punctuating
The scribbled page of common anguish.

Outside the window a workman climbs the scaffold
He winks and waves, the nurse pulls down the blind
But as it falls I glimpse in the far distance
A child running.

S.M. (1991)

The X-Ray Room

Doctor, doctor
With the fierce blue eyes
Gleaming from the glooming
Of his X-Ray room
All day he peers
Beneath the skin of others
For the shadow on the liver
The tumour on the kidney
The cancer in the lung
Never finding
What lies in the deep behind
His fierce blue eyes

M.Y. (1993)

Nil by Mouth

Whose command is this
Can stop her mouth to me,
Which other brazen lover
Has put up this board
Above her bed
To forbid entry to me
And reserve it for him?

Disguised in his white coat,
He can ask her to strip,
She will.
He can feel her breasts with his gloved fingers,
She will not shrink.
He can tell her to open her mouth,
She will

Nil kiss
Nil tongue
Nil mouth
Nil to him
I hate

M.Y. (1993)

Going Down

Any moment now I will be going down
– No obituary for me,
  no solemn memorial lecture –
To join not the illustrious but
  the anonymous dead.

There are so many more of us
  than you living,
Countless millions, bones stacked
  on bones
In those dark catacombs that stretch
Back to the beginning of time.

Down there I'll feast among old friends
  and relatives
Reclining on a stone sarcophagus
While cats and dogs and birds,
  my dear familiars
Prance overhead.

You must dance too, you living.
Dance and sing and tell good jokes
And love each other all you can.
Don't waste time sorrowing,
For you'll be joining us, alas,
  too soon,
In a moment you never thought would
  come so quickly
Dem bones, dem bones, dem dry bones
The hard rock band, banging their
  hollow drums

S.M. (1991)

Neighbours

We would walk together, my hand in hers,
Down the rows of Rest in Peaces, Much Loveds and Passed Overs,
Each of them from the same street
Now had a stone front door

I was from Number 29, I already knew that,
When she came to Doris and Jack Foster, the docker from
    Number 5,
Doris was her school friend from Number 9,
She knelt on the wet grass to prink up the plastic bloom

She told me that the neighbours
Who once had lived together
Were neighbours once again
To make it easy for them to find each other

She told me that people don't make new friends when they're dead
But they can keep old ones
The dead can comfort and protect each other
If they had known each other before

They also depended on her
They need to be talked to
By people who are still in their temporary homes
At Number 6, Number 10 and Number 29.

M.Y. (1990)

Cancer

Her sumptuous legs, promising so much,
Arresting other men's eyes to their appraisal
Kept me awake at night with hot imagining
Made me cry out from voluptuous dreams
Until one night she allowed my hand
To stroke them kindly and make them mine.

Her arms were other branches from the same tree
Stretching long and luscious from the same trunk.
I could blow my way up and down this downy surface
Like a tender zephyr
Bending down a thousand brown shoots
Before they sprang up straight again.

Now her arms are become twigs.
No longer concealed by those soft curves
Bones life never allowed me to see
Have disclosed the scaffold that was always waiting there
Her skin glows no more
Even the hairs do not bend to the breath.

Now the steroids swelling up her legs
Have made her flesh weep water
Enough to wet the carpet and my eyes.
But when I rub her thin thighs with oil of lavender,
Left to my own appraisal I love her more.
Behind the bones, alongside the crumpled skin
The same large brown eyes, larger now, shine out
As brightly as 35 years ago
When our souls first were joined together.

M.Y. (1993)

Body

What was so quiet a companion, my dumb friend,
Now cries out, groans, swells up with noxious fluid
Clamouring for attention.
Did I neglect you? Taking for granted
The ease with which you walked, breathed, ran for a bus?
We that were one, are two.
I bow before you.

S.M. (1993)

The Night Nurse

The night nurse arrives by taxi
A clumpy figure
When she takes off her coat
Underneath is the blue uniform of a nurse.
A sister with her badge of office,
The upside down hanging watch

She stops at the bottom of the stairs
To gather her strength
Before slowly she lifts her foot on to the first stair
Then another and another
All the while talking in a broken English.

After circling slowly round Sasha's bed
She fell back into her chair
Where she spent the night

M.Y. (1993)

And Next Week?

It would now be utmost joy
If under grey London skies
The streets spattered with litter
Gripping our arms tight
(She could still do that)
Sasha would hobble down the steps
Into the NHS wheelchair
To ride through our garden gate
Past the geraniums and the beercans
It was almost a daily outing

This week her muscles are so wasted she cannot move
She has almost hidden her pulse
Her hands are trembling.
While she is asleep,
Groaning a little now and then
Her open eyes are staring blind.
Her mouth is aghast
To suck in the gasps of air
Which is all her straining lungs can pump.
Last week, cannot I have last week again?

M.Y. (1993)

The Green Stone

You are one and indivisible,
Mary, Kittisaro, stone;
I hold the green stone in my hand
And I am holding your two hands in mine.

Flesh dissolves, withers, burns
In the flame,
Ashes on the surface of the water
like flower petals
Float downstream,
Our hands transformed to ashes;
Only the stone remains.

S.M. (1993)

Changing Places

How glad I was to hear your voice
Not by what you said
'My mouth will be wide open
It must be closed
When I die, when I die.'

My head is leaning against yours
My hand is cupping your chin
Not to make love again
But, still tenderly, to clamp your jaw shut
After you died, after you died.

Up till a moment ago before your head became a skull
An inch away on the other side of that soft skin
Your memories were ready to jump the gap
To put on the purple or the yellow dress
Before you died, before you died.

Hitler was there to circle around with Donne,
The scent of wallflowers on a summer's night,
The cry of seagulls swooping on the ferry,
The sharp taste of garlic in your father's house
While you were still alive, while still alive.

This verse shows I could not close your mouth
You can dance again in your purple dress
Between the continents in my not yet skull
You can cup your hands to catch my head
You are not yet dead, not yet dead.

M.Y. (1993)

The Company of the Birds

Ah the company of the birds
I loved and cherished on earth
Now, freed of flesh we fly
Together, a flock of beating wings,
I am as light, as feathery,
As gone from gravity we soar
In endless circles.

S.M. (1990)